ABOUT THE AUTHOR

Nafeesa Hamid is a British Pakistani poet and playwright based in Birmingham. She has been writing and performing for 6 years at events around the UK, featuring at nights such as Outspoken (London), Poetry is Dead Good (Nottingham), Find the Right Words (Leicester) and Hit The Ode (Birmingham). She was invited as a performer at TedxBrum 2016 (Power of Us). Nafeesa has also performed at Cheltenham and Manchester Literature Festivals as part of *The Things I Would Tell You: British Muslim Women Write*, a recent (2017) anthology publication by Saqi Books, edited by Sabrina Mahfouz. She is alumni of Mouthy Poets and Derby Theatre Graduate Associate Artists. She runs Twisted Tongues, an open-mic only poetry night at The Station in Kings Heath.

Nafeesa's poem 'Doctor's appointment' (featured here) was Highly Commended by the judges of the Forward Prize and appears in *The Forward Book of Poetry 2020*.

Twitter: @NafeesaHamid
www.facebook.com/nafeesa.hamid
https://vervepoetrypress.com/2018/05/10/nafeesa-hamid/

ABOUT BESHARAM

'*Besharam* is an outstanding collection from Nafeesa ... I think her poems are very special.' – **Imtiaz Dharker**

'Love this collection and finding it deeply affecting. The fearlessness is astonishing. Bravo!' - **Roz Goddard**

'Yesterday I read and was deeply moved by NafeesaHamid's debut, *Besharam*. Thank you Nafeesa for articulating so deftly and elegantly such complex material. I know I'll return to this book often.' - **Ruby Robinson**

'You know those times you pick up a poetry collection and read right the way through because every page is a grenade? ... *Besharam* is powerful, rebellious, tender and bold. I could not put this 'woman' down.' – **Hafsah Aneela Bashir**

'I love Nafeesa's vibrant, original and refreshingly original poems.' - **Josephine Corcoran**

'I highly, highly recommend Nafeesa's first book of poetry - *Besharam* - as this writer resonates on a whole other level.' - **Pam Reader**

'*Besharam* is staggering and heartbreaking. Absolute fire in the hand.' - **Anna Saunders**

Nafeesa Hamid
Besharam

VERVE
POETRY PRESS
BIRMINGHAM

PUBLISHED BY VERVE POETRY PRESS
Birmingham, West Midlands, UK
www.vervepoetrypress.com
mail@vervepoetrypress.com

FIRST PUBLISHED SEPT 2018
REPRINTED SEPT 2019

Reprinted and bound in the UK
by Imprint Digital, Exeter

ISBN: 978-1-912565-05-4

*For anyone who
is still finding
their way home.*

CONTENTS

Part 2: Mind

Part 3: Heart

Nafeesa introduces Mina Mekic, Yasmina Silva and Zeddie.

Acknowledgements.

FOREWORD

Nafeesa Hamid's debut collection is a necessary and potent meditation on the meaning of Womanhood, as witnessed through the eyes of a poet who has survived its most restrictive excesses but continues always to write forward. I agreed to collaborate in the collection as editor because I strongly believe that some stories must be nurtured, remembered and passed on.

As a girl of nine years old the poet was taken from the street outside her home and held hostage in a stranger's car for several hours, only being returned to her family on the morning of the following day. In those intervening hours the whole world changed. Grief, searching, loss and recrimination became her closest friends. *Besharam* suggests that on some cellular level Nafeesa is still lost in a stranger's car trying to remember the way home.

As a result, this whole book is a kind of hostage situation, and the kidnapping itself a metaphor for the condition of Woman in the 21st century. It is a therapeutic and personal collection, that veers from that defining moment into the universal symbols that mark the development of a girl child into a Woman body, and all that entails.

Honest, imagistic and at times surreal, we stand in the corner of the bedroom as she tries on woman body after woman body, finding that none of the bodies quite fit.

Divided into distinct Body and Mind sections *Besharam* attempts to name and own the two parts of each of us that we as women still have little agency over. The book finishes up with a Heart section that needs no words from me to understand and enjoy.

Read the book slowly and remember your own growing, or that of your sister, daughter, mother. Let her poems create poems within you.

Let this book be her homecoming.

Joelle Taylor, Editor, 2018

Besharam

Part 1: Body

Missing

My father walks from door to door,
hands held together like he is doing dua.
They are covered in blood.
He splutters
'beti' to anyone who will listen,
blood spraying from his grieving mouth.
He is covered in blood,
Jummah salwaar kameez
bleached white before.
(I wonder how my mother got out the stains.)
A blood vessel has erupted
and my father thinks he is beyond repair.

I wonder if my mother bothered scrubbing the stains out
or if she buried the whole thing instead.

...

My mother is a suburban English village;
quiet and collected,
she has not made a sound yet,
Tasbeeh *against her chest.*

I think me and my mother found Womanhood that day.

In her absence
and in mine
I felt like she was praying to me.
I heard her words as clear as the call to prayer on a Friday afternoon,
yet the congregation sat at home and wept.
The muazzin *answers questions from police.*

Later I find out she was praying
for me.
She rebirthed me that night
as part jawan, *part still child, still nine.*
The string of her tasbeeh beads is fraying

with the dampness of her hands.
Her blooming chest has lost count of the
Alhamdulilah
and SubhanAllah
and Allahu Akbar's

but here she is,
still praying for my return.

Body

This body is woman. Grown woman. Doesn't wet the bed anymore, Mother, woman. Ready to baby, woman. Will not fetch her brother his drink, woman. This body is touched like woman. This mouth is all woman with its no-thank you's and dryness and gobbled up greed dreams of wanting to write about being woman.

Your first girl

When my mother birthed me, I wonder if
she smiled. Or thought about chores instead.
I wonder if she hugged me that night, the
next day, a week later in secret, in the
middle of the wheat fields, at the side of her
bed, in the middle of the night. Her first girl.
So much trouble to be born with this girl.

Passport photo

In Big Mom's kitchen,
in the cupboard with the tea and sugar and cardamoms,
you'll find a small passport photo of baby me
sellotaped on the left.
A tiny, screaming, alien toddler -
slightly resembling Frankenstein's monster.
A tiny, alien me
ready
to fly over to England
for a better life.

Sisters

My little sister is 10. When we leave the house, my mother says to her *put on a longer dress!* My father says *where is her scarf? Where is your scarf, girl?*
They are getting her ready to woman when her woman body is still curled up foetal, like, let me sleep forever. Her belly and cheeks plump with Girl, with reading Jaqueline Wilson and experimenting with the neon pink free lipstick from Girl Magazine; she is not ready to woman, with her cherry peaked breastlets, her ears unpierced, unsexed. I do not want her to ever woman. She is already looking for the power of woman and my parents are already telling her that woman needs no power. Has no power. When she was born they were telling me the same. My body is no place for man, no place for me to woman like woman, like

real woman.

Let me start again.

I am 10 and my only wish is for a sister. Preferably older. Her name would be Nabeela.
[I'm jealous enough not to see the shift in my parent's hands – no one flinches in the house anymore.]

I read Girl magazine, wish for a sister to teach me how to experiment with neon pink. She is becoming *woman*. Perhaps she is already more woman than I ever was at 10. We will never show mother our unfurling pomegranate bodies – hold on to your seeds, girls.

My little sister is already looking for the power of woman and
I'm grinding down the idea right in front of her eyes

telling her to keep running, keep running, we just need to keep
running, kid.

Our bodies are no place for us.

Hijab

This woman body once liked the way her
hair sat beneath her hijab. Hair tucked in,
she experiments folding the fabric to fit
her face – to hide eyebrows or not? She
decided to wear her new-found pride on
the first day of Year 7. Her father said, *of
course she should!* Her mother said *Of course
you will – you're a woman now. Don't you
know?*

Shades of woman

She tells me I look like sex tonight. Really, you do, can't you
see it? And when I look down I do see; I see my breasts plump
and hairless flung out of my sex dress like sleeping strays. I
know this body is woman. This body is power; awake, alive.
Paint me red and call me the devil. Let my curves shape waves
to ricochet off your eyeballs. Give me permission, or don't.
What does it matter? Listen to every word; this shade of
lipstick is perfect.
This shade of woman is perfect; delicious, Pakistani mango
sweet. Eat me ripe. Lick lips, smack teeth, kisses, swallow, spit.
They say I'm as guilty as the days are long. All my seventy
billion shades of red cannot save me, heal me, from the
sickness of being woman.

First time

This woman body cannot remember the first time she saw dick. Maybe she does and won't say. Maybe she can't say because it was dark in the back of his car and his blue jeans were unzipped, but the flesh he flashed was probably just leg. She closed her eyes anyway.

Illness

This body is man crawling out through woman. Woman clawing to find man in her fat, not-quite-size-10 thighs and 36 I'm-not-quite-sure-I'm-a-B-cup-anymore breasts. This is woman. It is all over me, a disease I was born to catch for offending Mother Nature – the Devil – in another life. The way my hands burn when I touch this woman body of mine is a sure sign woman is a work of the devil – is ill. My woman body is ill. I am all striped thighs, arms slashed deep enough for woman to feel like something, like more than woman herself, more than woman alone, lonely woman. This woman body has been made to love, to withstand man with all his hate, to soften him and his offspring. There is too much love in this woman body.

Porn stash

This woman body burned karahi oil red when her Mother
found the porn stash.
She did not explain that she just wanted to know what she was
growing up to be and whether or not her vagina was normal.
She did not know vaginas from pussies back then.

Blame

This woman body did not flinch with
regret when she told her mother she
blamed her. This woman body did not cry
after the slap. She just stood red, in her
woman skin, unmoved. Unapologetic.

What she is for you

This woman body does not know how to twirl her frigid hips to music, only to men who will ask no questions about who she is, what she likes, where she was born, whom to and what she loves. Maybe she likes feeling like a dirty rag, like the dirtiest pages of those dirty, Western magazines her father used to sell. This woman body does not need to be told it is clean, pure, Virgin-smothered silk. Because it does not feel like it ever has been and so she asks God to forgive the misfortune of being Woman that He blessed her with.

Night off

Do you know this woman body, the body of this woman with her lubricated secrets hand-wrapped for the nine-year-old girl who lay in the back seat of his car begging to see her mother? Do you know this woman body that does not fit into size small salwar kameez anymore, only into the baggyness of her Western world? She struts into gay bars these days, all sexed up with sizzling flesh and dark eyes, her glittered body dripping away fat in the heat. She leans at the bar and smiles, thinking God can't see her being woman here. This woman body decides not to think about God tonight.

Her

This woman body sees this other woman in a way where she can only wonder how the hell she does it so damn well. Woman feels in a way she is not supposed to. She watches her rock back in her chair and enjoys her wide smile and her grey, gold-tipped eyes for a moment that's not long enough to feel guilty about later. She hears those click-clack, clattering keys speed and slow in time with her mind, she feels the last few letters being pushed down, feels herself being pushed, pushed, pushed ... and then she knows to stop feeling like this because click-clack clattering keys are even against her ears as she sleeps. This ain't right, she thinks; imagine she knew. She'd hate you.

First date

When you had me up against that tree in
Ward End Park, our noses melting into
each other in the cold, my school blazer
crumpled on the frozen grass, the cold
air from your mouth forcing me back
into the tree, and you jokingly
threatened to rape me, I knew then I was
not ready to woman.

You are everything against nature

When you knifed him, you did not feel like woman, did you?
You did not feel you could ever baby with all this Man inside of
you. This was not how to woman.

Two girls having a conversation on a step outside a church

Are you? I don't know. Do you think you are? I'm just in love with her though. It's just her. It's just her. It's just her. Just her.

Upon finding your daughter

Pulled up from
the pavement on
Cotterills Lane crying,
by strange women
with kind faces.
They tell Girl
it'll be okay.
Inside their home,
her mother tumbles
through door, falls
at feet – pink
scarf throttling around
her neck – unashamed.
Eyes bloodshot sockets,
noosed hair hitting
against her face.
Father follows slow
and soft like
he has seen
and known death.
He tries to
smile, but cries
over head of
Girl instead. He
fathers. They Speak
with strange voices.
Girl does not
listen, but hears.

Man of the house

Aunty tells me they used to woman by
shoving pencils down the sides of
sofas, passing notes because He wouldn't
let them talk. I watch Him now and He
stills sits in the same corner of the room,
still watching, through older eyes, still
conducting silence in this room, all these
years later as me and my siblings sit
twiddling our thumbs in front of Him on
Eid day.

Mum's Spicy Chicken

Rumble. Grumble. Rumble.
Splash, stroke, thrust
and rest.
I'm thinking she probably doesn't want to touch me;
she looks at me with blank eyes,
too full with other thoughts
for me to be seen.
She's bored of this lifetime routine.
Chop, cut, chop, chop, cut –
I don't bleed.
Spark – it doesn't light up so she tries again.

Spark.
Flame. Thump, sizzle.
My skin tightens around my body,
anaemic legs burn in the heat.
My insides loosen up.
She swings me on to my back,
prods her finger down my spine;
grunts.
I'm picked out, well-browned; just how they like me.
Brown on the outside, pink on the inside.
A cultural mish-mash.

The boys rush to greet me,
grab me by my leg and slap me
on to their plates;
my sweat already congealing their fingers.
The boys like me;
their eyes all bright and empty like hers.

They tear off my crackling coat
and dig teeth into my flesh
which falls off with ease.
The boys like me
when I'm well-browned
and have stopped sizzling
and am silent.

Like a virgin

Do you know about surgical hymen reconstruction?
Women from all over the world pay from $600 to become virgins again. To become respectable again. To become clean again. To have men love them. Love them properly. Or at all. Surgical hymen reconstruction means women can become the type of women that men want them to be - whole, sweet fruit still encased, intact, skin tightly protecting what was only meant for Man.

Even her spit say sex
(After *Defence* by Jamila Woods)[10]

Girl touch turn
Everyone soft
Her sultry temptress
Medusa or siren/
Her red lips
Suspicious/ boy
Frisks every bump

Girl in bed
Be like girl
On street corner or
Girl on dance table
Girl brush teeth spit
Even her spit
Say sex.

Her a walking
Casualty/ whole
Body asking for it

Predator/ sinner

---

[10] The BreakBeat Poets, New American Poetry
in the Age of Hip-Hop (2015)

The in-between date

I shaved until I was newborn for this guy.

Curled my hair cute behind my ears as my parents slept in the next room. Sprayed the Isi Miyaki that was saved for special occasions like Eid, across neck, wrists, anywhere else I could imagine his mouth, hands, tongue forging their place. Nivea moisturise peach-peel skin. Baggy t-shirt free from the National Lottery and pyjama shorts.

You creep into the garden turned on harder by the adrenaline of being found out; your brother is sleeping only meters away. You have left the back door unlocked. The boy who walks through the back gate is ginger, Reebok traccies and smiling with glaze-eyed testosterone. His hands, both, are dragging themselves up your chest finding something to hold on to, finding ripened nipples and making do, pinching and pulling you into him, your pyjama shorts limping unwillingly in the night's rain asking you what the hell you're doing. He moves one hand down and you move yours down and he's as hard as your dad's knuckles against your cheek when you were seven and you're as wet as your mother's tears when they found you at 5am when you were nine. And he is moving faster and you are moving faster and it is raining over both of you but who the fuck cares.

Yes. Yes. Yes.

He takes his yes other hand off your sore yes bloated yes breasts yes and slithers down yes and down yes and down yes and he's trying to push himself into your tight wetness yes and you are no panicking now no and mumbling no something about virgin no not done this no virgin please stop I'm a virgin stop please no stop. And he does.

You offer a blowjob instead. You go to bed still tasting of semen and sin, fighting the urge to chisel away the insides of your mouth. I shaved until I was newborn for this guy. I feel soft and old and torn and worn now. I do not reply to any of his Facebook messages. I do not answer his questions about who I want to be when I grow up.

I just want to stop being so woman.

How men are made

Perhaps this is how men are made.
Perhaps he was more man than fist.
Perhaps she closed her eyes
instead of glaring into his like an insolent
child.
Perhaps she sunk her knuckles into the
leathery skin of sofa
rather than his face.

The Ramadan calendar is four years out
of date and still no one will take it down.

In a freeze frame we all look bored more
than we do tense, more than we do scared,
more than we do broken.

In awkward angles
we are waiting for him to kick her balloon
belly,
waiting for her to scream, fall to floor,
crawl towards door,
waiting for someone to stop them,
waiting to wake up,
waiting for God to answer all the prayers
we made up in the madness,
waiting for my brother to cry but still look
like man in his five-year-old skin.

Because real men watch, they don't walk
waiting for her to bruise,
keep asking for more – her mouth wide
awake in this frame
she will not shut up
waiting for him to tell us he is a
hard-working man,
hard-working father and husband –
he is not monster.

He is my father.

Perhaps this is how men are made.

School assembly

(1)It is only the second week of year 4 and everyone is still trying to fit in summer stories before the morning bell.

(2) My father walks with me through floating sea of staring eyes. For once, he is on time, and for once, I am too distracted to be ashamed of his socks/ sandals combo and his unironed shirt with a missing button down the middle. My head teacher escorts us to her office like a prison guard. I lag behind pretending I'm not with them.

(3) How did this happen?

(4) I wonder how she found out.

(5) I don't know what the point of this meeting is. Why she couldn't have just sent a letter. Why I had to be there.

(6) In her office, she smiles too wide in a very un-teachery sort of way. It doesn't feel right. She doesn't look right. None of us look right, hanging on to our chairs, ready to run. My father is being overly polite. I answer too quick, fire out single word bullets aimed for her gawping, sympathetic mouth. I want to be in class. Or eaten whole.

(7) There will be an assembly. She has a Duty of Care. She keeps saying that bit; DUTY OF CARE.

In assembly people stare once I am sat down. Whispers reverberate across the hall – I bounce on the vibrations from the polished wood floor and keep staring at my pink velcro trainers with the flashing lights. I scratch the velcro. Head Teacher brings up The Incident. Everyone is silent. (Boy) picks his nose next to me. (Girl) plaits (Girl's) hair next to me. I feel the stares burning through my scalp. Scratch velcro.

(8) Our first Stranger Danger talk. Lessons are learned. She tries her best not to look over at me.

(9) We stand up in our class rows and walk back to class with heavier shoulders – big things on minds of small people.
(10) In the playground I am nested by a mob of over-excited, well-meaning girls who were ears open for the best gossip the school had ever had. I chew through the sour fruit, choke on the pit.

Girl

When I was a girl I never learned to swim or ride a bike. I wet
the bed a lot. I got taken once and returned mostly in pieces. I
once told my father to fuck off -
he left me in a pool of my own piss for being bad. My mother
once came to my bed and gave me a Snickers bar after a
beating. She did not say anything about the bloody man
imprint on my forehead.

Penny the Magic Bunny

Penny has disappeared.
Penny does not know how to get back.
The audience are getting agitated.
Where the fuck are you Penny?
Penny has fucked up the trick.

Nafeesa the Magic Student

Nafeesa has disappeared.
Nafeesa does not know how to get back.
The lecturers are getting agitated.
Where the fuck are you Nafeesa?
Nafeesa has fucked up university
Nafeesa has fucked up her life.

Instruction manual on giving birth

Make sure the father is in the room.
He
will
watch.
Don't tell your parents -
you're probably not married yet.
I've heard you can ask for all the drugs you like.

Remember to smile when the midwife -
who is pretty and blonde and wears expensive rimless glasses -
hands you your child.
Remember the child is yours.
Remember to thank Allah.
And apologise at the same time.

Morning after

The hoody that you wore on New Year's
Eve smells of booze and cigarettes and
it smells of that boy and every moment
in which you made out. You lay in bed,
spread out and bare, thinking about how
this Morning After The Night Before is
just the fucking best.

Teeth

My mouth is a fish, agape,
when talking to you;
I do not hear anything I'm saying.
I awkwardly ask about your day
and you, without a care,
tell me
and then ask about mine.
I fiddle with the microwave,
avoid eye contact, turn my back to you
pretend to fold away dish-cloths,
putting dirty ones back in the cupboard,
the steam from your boiling pot is making my back
itch

and this entire charade is spilled like red wine across carpet
(I am not a slut because I didn't say no)
this entire charade is gummy
(I am not a slut because I couldn't say no)
this is stained teeth and bad breath,
tongue drilled into mouth
this is far from tongue and cheek,
hands harassing thighs
(I don't know why I didn't say no)
crooked necks,
reggae blasting from my laptop,
the battery is dying – someone should probably charge it -
bodies against each other like grinding teeth
or screeching chalk
or like bulldozers tearing down homes

I am turning stone
I am stone
I have become dust between your fingers.
I wish I'd said no.
Does the 'no' matter?
Did it then?
Does it now?

How alone do you feel post-sex?

The sun is up and you
haven't slept.
You want to pray away last night's sins,
but the boy is still beside you,
at peace,
he is sleeping
or dead,
you don't care,
not really.

Have you ever felt so alone after sex that you
read Warsan Shire's
men in cars
to feel more human,
less like yourself,
to picture other endings
with all these
men,
to dissect your own behaviours
until they are nothing but your own
guilt.
You are always swathed in
guilty;
slut red.
God's name is tar on your tongue this morning.

Back seats

I find you on the back seats
of every car I get into,
spread,
more woman skin
than fits over your
pre-pubescent body,
kicking the passenger seat
like the child you could have been.

I mourn every part of you,
thick curls piled up in a pony,
lilac salwaar kameez,
summer sandals -
flowers starting to curl upwards, the white is turning grey -
you smell of stale piss and men's hands
that were only made to hunt you.
You still smell of stale piss
but also of your mother,
and you hope
that she will sniff you out
and scold you
and force you to take a bath
even after all these years.

Ice cream

My house mate tells me
that all this sex is getting out of hand.
Promiscuity only leads to emptiness.

You will be left hollow,
all your woman scooped out,
you begin as the sweetest of ice creams
but all that is now left of you
is a stale wafer,
half chewed,
soggy,
thrown over a shoulder
for the rest of the 'gulls.

Dough

Morning.
Colgate toothpaste.
Chairs.
Sat on sofa.
Handmade covers - satin.
Rough with age and too many arses.
Bobbles hanging off,
ready to dive into the interrogation.

Mum was cooking lassi ka saag yesterday.
That was the night before.

People. Customers. shop.

Police officer. Woman.

The police officer came to throw dirt in the burn wound.
Our house stills smells of hot roti from the night before.

Mum must have pounded that dough until there was
roti flour all over the house,
the street,
Alum Rock,
the whole of Birmingham,
sitting on eyelashes,
making people cough,
screen wipers on cars jam or even break
because of it -
all this flour.

The police officer came to throw dirt
in the burn wound,
she wanted to retain the juices that otherwise might
drip, drip away.
I just wanted to cook the leavened dough
that had been exposed
to too much air already,
and eat it all up,
swallow it whole,

but the police officer didn't want to leave it
to rest.
she wanted to pick through the grains
and bring back the baker.

Giving her away

From daughter to *dhulan*
with the swipe of a father's hand over her head,
Bismillah,
you are someone else's problem now.

Tracing steps into the loneliness of it all

In the back of his car,
She watches the night sky,
the moon and stars,
face hanging out of the window,
a broken lamp,

a girl, the man in the moon, the car, A Man and God.

She feels like an abandoned car park

when he reaches to touch the grenade between her legs.

If a tree falls in the woods and no one is around to hear it
did it actually happen?

And then she is sat cross legged
in that uphill forest
where he told her home was.

Back on to mud,
grass in ears,
skin crunching over summer leaves.
It's colder than she expected,
even for a midsummer's night,
but she doesn't flinch in the dirt
like I thought she would.
Just eyes closed, lips stitched,
hands fingering through earth until the cringe
of dirt beneath nails has passed.

There are crickets reading prayers
in her ears
and spiders
who only come out at this time
to build webs over forgotten settlements.

She lets them build home over her most intimate areas
because she was never really afraid of them anyway.

Part 2: Mind

Women who cry

This woman body does not cry. Not even when it's left alone,
in dark double-bed alone. Not even into the back of man. Not
into the sloped neck holes of other woman; she womans too
much and womans too close and it makes this woman body
feel shame, feel alone in her sole, womanly shame. She
watches Coronation Street and waits for them to tell her when
to cry. She watches depressing films about kids with no homes,
kids on the run and beaten wives and abused kids and starving
kids and lost men and she waits for them all

to tell her when to cry. She womans like this woman body of
mine. I cry about the state of my woman.

About being too little woman.

Too much.

Doctor's appointment

My mind is all woman. It is uneasy. My doctor tells me part of my woman is ill. I don't want to woman anymore, I tell him. He nods without looking at me. His glasses do not budge from the tip of his nose as he continues to take notes. He asks how long. I say since my mother birthed me and named me Woman. He asks how long. I say too long. He says the new tablets will help me woman again.

Paperweight

This woman mouth collapses when I ask her what's wrong.
Woman does not know why she cannot woman properly in
this world. Why she stops fighting like woman at least once a
day, puts the weight of woman down and says *'fuck off. Go find
someone else to carry you. I don't want to do this anymore.'*

Summer storm

Woman stands in summer storm with a high vis jacket and no umbrella. Rain drops are catching and collecting on the front peak of her hijab, then dropping and sliding down the sides of her face to form a beard at her chin. The playground is empty today, silent - the trees are still and watching with breath held at woman who is now bent double under the monkey bars, knees folded against chest, crunching her foiled fate against her unholy body, ready to be unwomaned.

Woman as a McDonald's Happy Meal balloon

Being woman is like being this McDonald's Happy Meal balloon in the middle of the four-lane traffic. It wants to get hit, doesn't get hit, changes its mind and bobs away to the edge, at the railing, wondering how to get itself out of this mess. She is stood playing footsy with her own feet at the edge of the four lane, wondering how to get out of this mess.

Funfair in the bathroom

On the faltered arrogant tiles
on the empty storm bath
on the blunt porcelain toilet
on the cracked cold sink
on the open bridled cupboard
on the abandoned Lush soap
on the jagged tongued razor
on the prickly old toothbrush

you left the scent of thunder stuck on our skin,
you heaved the heavens out from your shattered insides
and around you a collision
of pills, water and vomit.

You are blathered across the tiles,
ears ringing
from the new door being kicked in.
Toes curled in on themselves, afraid,

the smell is putrid and old -
haven't we done this
time and time again?

Someone is asking
if you have vomited yet.

Your mouth is congealed,
slug like slime gluing your lips shut,
throat dry, fists clenched, love lost,
save yourself, save each other, let someone in,
there is help on the way, just hold on, just hold on.

If the new door is knocked down who will pay for the door?

You never really think about the impact of your behaviour on
others
do you?
You hear lightning shock voices outside the door, but still don't
move.
You still lay silent
and spinning;
merry-go-round
ferris wheel
spinning cups -
this is *some* fair.
And we keep spinning.

Putting out fires

When your house is burning down, get a hose, call the fire services, shout and scream – put that shit out. Don't count on just spitting on the fire to put it out.

Candyfloss

On the second day of the Leaving Dad story
my mother stood in big mom's living room ripping tendrils
of hair out
like candyfloss.

She said the walls were trying to eat her.

Those disgusting, nauseating peach walls.
She said
the walls
were trying
to
eat
her.

'Get away, get away, get away from me all of you!'

Big mom tells me to go upstairs.

Upstairs I get a single, sharp 3B pencil
and sketch a door handle
with shaking hands, anger pulsating through my forehead,
vision blotted.

The next day my art teacher congratulates me on my
abstract form -
he hasn't covered that yet.

Last Legs

My father and I walk through hospital corridors;
he looks ahead,
I look at how my shoes change over the years -
black patent school, white Barbie trainers, dolly's, black velvet
adult, converse runners.

The clinical, squeaky floor stays the same.
The smell of shit food and death smells the same.

Our arms rub against parallel walls.
We are silent
in all the years spent
walking up and down hospital corridors -

me and my dad
sniffing up other people's dinner menus and fluffy tears.
We wait for the bodies that move too slow now.
They wind down.
Neither of us stares.

Riding the wave

When the doctor visits he says I seem distracted. He asks what the voices are saying. My tongue turns into a lead weight so I leave the room to drink some water and when I wake up I am back at work re-stocking Pink Himalayan Sea Salt that my house mate keeps stealing. People keep telling me that things will get better. It's inevitable. In therapy I learn about 'Riding the Wave' - nothing lasts forever, including emotions. We just need to ride the wave, reach peak, see them through. Nothing lasts forever. I still love you.

Change

The Aloe Vera handwash has nearly finished.
The flowers are long dead.
The black jumper is gathering bobbles.
I forget to wear the ring you gave me.
The mementos from my cork board are falling off.
Nobody is putting them back up.
Do you feel
better yet?
The plant has started to walk, no,
water itself.
The bedsheets have finally been changed.
There are too many pictures of me in my room.
The Weetabix has been occupied.
The last of the toothpaste is gone.
There are too many pictures of me in my room.

What to pack when you're about to be sectioned under the Mental Health Act. Again.

1. All of the socks you can find.
2. One, and only one, wired bra that you will instantly regret wearing anyway.
3. Your notebook in case you meet someone in hospital who also likes hearing sad poetry.
4. A pack of 20 Sterling. Superkings, of course.
5. Your sanity so you can get back out again.
6. A razor
tucked in the waistband of your jeans. The nurses won't understand that as an Asian woman hair growth is alarmingly fast, so you feel the need to shave every day and do not want to be watched doing this mundane task every day.
7. A pocket sized photo of you and your recent ex
8. More pants than you will ever need in your entire fucking life
9. Jewelry and makeup in case there is a party on ward
10. A towel
11. One pair of jeans but all the t-shirts
12. Patience. You will really, really, really need that shit.
13. Your medication or a list of the meds you're on
14. Your phone charger. All other ligature items packed at the top of your bag because they'll be taken away first.
15. Your sanity. Things will get better. You will be out before Christmas. Or New Years. Or your birthday. Or before that important event you're supposed to be performing at.
16. A book of Durood Shareef. Your faith in God will be restored.

17. The love of those you didn't hurt this time.

18. Your rational head.

19. A plant cutting gift from your housemate. He annoys you, but he is currently fighting with nurses, police, doctors and a social worker to get you un-sectioned. Or to give you time to understand what's going on.

20.   Your parent's words: *sabr. Sabr. Sabr.*

Food: a relationship

Do you
want to eat
today?

Do you think you
should
eat today?

Can I eat today?

Am I allowed
to eat
today?

Should I eat?
I don't know.

Who will die
if I eat something today?

Eat
eat eat

Don't you dare have anything to eat today.
But what about -
No.

I really shouldn't.

Do you want to

EAT

today?

Will I eat?
How many bites?

Fuck you.
Fuck food.

Can I eat now,
please?

Can I eat
you?

I need you to stop
eating me.
I need you to stop eating me now.

I do not want to eat today.

Demolition

The demolition of my home began just before Christmas:
a flyer stuck in my mouth,
'Call this number if you have any queries',
and that's it.
Bulldozers begin by tearing down my bedroom first:
I stand and watch from my workplace,
I am numb but remember to keep calm,
show them you are being rational.
When I edge nearer to the site,
I am met by men in uniforms
who will not explain why
it is my home they have chosen,
I am struck dumb.
There are weeds in the front garden that I am most
concerned about
and also my plants on the windowsill
that the men in uniform did not think to salvage.
I worry about how my manager will react
when I tell him
my home has been destroyed.
Will he let me keep my job at the store?
The ones in charge complain that they have been waiting
hours for my return,
that the process cannot be reversed,
that the paperwork has gone through,
that if I had complied when they had visited in the morning,
maybe they could have left my living room standing,
perhaps even the kitchen.

But I have never been good with compromising,
I am greedy,
I want what is mine to myself,
my home, that is.
When I go up to my room to chuck my possessions into
a single rucksack,
I am dizzy,
partially because my life is falling apart,
partially because of the brick dust that is floating about
my room,
choking me -
an ironic representation of the system that I am stuck in,
where standing up for your rights looks like insanity.

Lonely

Why so lonely, girl?
Are you scared
that you will set on fire
and burn,
burn down to find there is nothing of you left
to be saved by anyone,
let alone those who are there desperate to save you,
to pick you up and shake you inside out
until you are no more nonsense,
'better' than ever.
Little girl, you do not need saving.
You do not need piecing back together,
you are not a jigsaw,
so rub that fear out your eyes
and dance only for yourself
and dance yourself well,
dance yourself home,
arms akimbo, two left legs as well as two left feet,
muttering made up lyrics
to Dawn Penn
shouting the few words that you did remember,
on your own, alone, but not lonely.

Crisis

You are glued to the safety of the armchair in your room,
body curled into velvet arms,
clothes strewn across the carpet in an urgent attempt to
find ground,
lights out,
you have only ever found comfort in darkness.
You play over what you might say to the crisis team
- that's if you can find the bit of paper with their number
scribbled on and forgotten –

'Hello Jane. I am worried about the glow coming from the far corner
of my bedroom.
The bottle of vodka is shattering against the glass of my head.,
I have put a bin over my head to muffle out
The Commandments.
I am not ready to be
messiah, Jane.
There are snakes hissing and vines twisting,
metal bending itself into exits,
little running green men wearing white coats
dashing across my periphery.
Jane, will you come here and open the window to let them out,
to let me out?
Jane can you let me out
or bring me in
or hold me close or
slap me out of this
mess?'

The glow in the far corner of the room
is no longer in the far corner of the room now
but swallowing me.
I realise it is sunlight
I am doused in
and not death.

Lovers

I scare you off
with talk about the 'other' in my life.
You are jealous
of the amount of time I spend -
every waking and unconscious moment -
on appeasing my other half.
We're not in an official relationship.
The way we fight figures otherwise.

You're scared off when I mention hospital visits,
sectioning, my opinion on the health service crisis.
You don't want to know,
you don't want me to hurt you,
- hurt is a strong word -
you don't want me to swallow you whole,
you don't want to be left
fragmenting my mind and body
back together,
you don't want the man-handling of me,
we are too tired for this shit,
I remind you of your mother
or ex-girlfriends,
you are terrified of all my Womaness,
breasts too big, hips too wide, mind too mad.
I watch what I say around you now.

After you've gone

When you're gone
they'll say
'I can't believe it. She looked so well.'
She was doing so well.
We didn't see it coming.
Was she praying, do you know?

They'll sip through straws at my funeral,
the men will wail uncontrollably, inconsolable,
the women will carry my casket,
to showcase to the men in the other room
at Ghamkol Sharif,
not a single tear shed from the women,
they did all they could.
There are those who will be angry,
crunch teeth, tongues bitten to blood,
arms folded away from hugs and opinions.
People will keep saying how they are
shocked.
This is awful,
what an awful thing
to happen
to someone
so young.
The women will carry the casket
on shoulders as strong as the foundations of homes,
heads focussing on feet,
on the closest point to God.

Focussing on God
and the unfairness of it
all.
How brown girls are abused
over and over.
How no one cares.

In this poem I am the atomic bomb

My mother will lay face down on the sofa
(that is too big for the living room, too big for the house now,
too big to hold her close
enough)
she will remain there for years.
My father's nose will become a burst dam
of blood
he will finally sell the shop.
My brother's will become mute.
Wholesome, round sorry's for mouths.
My youngest brother will stumble
and fall
into his man skin, for a second time too soon
(real men watch, they don't walk).

My sister. My sister. My sister.

My parent's say friends come and go,
but my friends will haunt the house
with their stories of me,
linger in corners crying
or trying to make themselves useful,
trying to understand,
their bodies clinking like the china in my mother's cupboard
which is only taken out on special occasions.
My therapist will lean out of health clinic windows, smoking,
and blow bubbles in his office until 5pm –
he is being mindful in breaking,
before going back to his own family,

throwing down his briefcase,
throwing down his arms and legs
collapsing on his newly tiled kitchen floor
And whispering
'I love you'
or gratitude for the lives around him
until the cows come home.
These people will never leave you or
hurt you
or disappoint
in the ways I did.

I have been laying face down in my bed for hours now,
my wires twisted
no one knows how to unplug me
how to defuse this bomb,
dismantle my body
into something more safe,
more living than alive,
less likely to explode
into the faces of those there
right at the front.

New beginning

I am crawling back into my mother's womb,
drenched in amniotic fluid
an event,
finding a home within home,
I will beg her to take me back,

to *chadars* swept over faces,
pestle and mortar hands.
I will promise to be better
this time around,
less girl,
more woman,
coriander seeds crushed within palms,
rubbed until the scent
has flared up my nostrils,
star and moon, *sabz aur safedh*
glowing from my chest.
I would cross all the mountains of Mirpur to
belong to my mother again.
I will not complain about wringing out clothes by hand,
or scrubbing floors on Saturday mornings,
or crying out onions mixed with slaps,
or wearing salwaar kameez
that at one time
felt more ugly step sister
than Cinderella.

That shame is now swallowed as quick
as memooni biryani at Eid,
or apologies for all those times I...

I will promise to be better
this time around.
I will not tear through you.
Instead I will rebirth myself softly
and quietly.
I will not disturb anyone.
I will not break promises.
I swear I will be more woman this time around.

2003

I lost my mind
somewhere on the A38 back to Birmingham,
back to Alum Rock,
back to my mother,
back to Kulfi sticks on lazy Sunday evenings in front of ITV.
I lost my mind,
found it swept behind the chewed up sofa we dragged
from Alderson road,
alongside the decrepit body of a lifeless nine-year-old,
forgotten.

I lost my mind in the haziness of the summer of 2003.
The scent of moth-balls is nauseating,
reminds me of strange men in strange cars.

Jinn

She's ill you know,
(she needs professional help)
always has been
a quiet child,
(an introvert)
woh mandhi rehthi.
(trauma does that)
she's had *nazar* done on her
(did you forget to say *'MashaAllah'* that one time?)
Leave her be, she bites you know,
blow prayers over her before sleep,
the Jinns rest beneath her bed
the imam will give her blessed water,
splash it over her face,
over her bed,
she is drowning, thinks she might be stuck in a car, but
abi zam zam will be sure to fix her,
get the Jinn out by its throat
until we are nothing but sorrys
swept up by zam zam water.

In this one no one notices

In this one no one notices
how time has ground itself into dust,
how a lost brown girl
was just that -
a lost brown girl.
No one will notice
that the Weeping Fig
and Madagascan Dragon Tree
and Purple Hearts
had dried out weeks ago,
how the glasses with vodka mixers
had gathered dead flies and dust,
how ripped out hairs and split ends became carpet,
how the lamp was never switched off,
how the curtains had not moved in months,
their lips as tightly bound
as her limbs to bed,
how the bin overflowed with diabetes,
how the blue glow from the laptop
had tinged her skin.
No one notices how
the mirror had cracked,
the flowers in her vase dried out to a crisp,
because in this one
we are representing fragility,
how vulnerability is ugly,
how cows do come home,
how chickens do come home to roost.

How we all just want
something or someone or somewhere
to call home.
In this one no one notices
that the brown girl
does not return home.

Part 3: Heart

In this section of *Besharam* I would like to introduce you to three of the most exciting voices on the Birmingham poetry scene, whose work I respect and love, and who I hope will one day get the recognition they deserve. Their work is both brave and bold, exploring issues from social inequality to femininity to love and relationships. Watch these womxn rise and listen to their every word; they will be creating waves across our city.

Amina Mekic is a 17 year old aspiring Bosnian writer based in Birmingham. I first met Mina at Verve Poetry Festival where I saw her perform an almighty set with a quiet confidence. After two years of underground writing, she has recently been sharing her work at events such as Hit the Ode and Poetry Jam (Birmingham) as well as compiling her own collection of poems. She aims to challenge traditional femininity in her own culture whilst incorporating the natural imagery that is prominent in her homeland. Her work is a reflection of her transition into adulthood as a teenager and the emotions she faces on the way.

Yasmina Silva is a final year student of Political Economy at the University of Birmingham. An aspiring author, spoken word poet and all time afro centrist and feminist. She writes a lot about injustice and is also learning to write more personally. She comes from a little known country called Guinea Bissau which she plans on highlighting on everyone's map. Yasmina is an extraordinarily powerful performer, and it is wonderful to watch the way she becomes her poems when she recites them from memory on the stage. She has a stirring, precise yet passionate way with words.

Zeddie is a community developer at Free Radical, part of the Beatfreeks Collective. Zeddie's work is largely cathartic, giving not only her, but also readers/ listeners hope and relief during darker days when mental health is playing up. While she describes herself as a theatre maker, producer and facilitator – and her theatre work is truly wonderful – I think she is an amazing poet and I am thrilled that she has agreed to be included here. Without a doubt, Zeddie is a huge asset to our city and the arts; a change maker.

Nafeesa

Strings - *Mina Mekic*

On the checklist of the people you will meet,
He will be one of the people you will 'love'

The boy that comes with 'no strings attached'
     other than those pulling at your heart, operating you as if
     you were a puppet, he makes you weak at the knees
Every time he grins or makes a spineless joke,
     you will support him blindly out of 'love'
pure, blind, hopeful love: the dangerous kind
that lets the mind wander and leaves any form of judgement
     clouded

Once you submit yourself in an attempt to break him, he will
make sure that there are no strings left;
He will use those callous hands
     Slide the last string down those milky thighs which
     inspire his explicit mind
And
You will feel the cold
     It will run up your body and seep into your skin
     It will freeze the 'love' in your veins
     It will melt loves warmth and condense your vision
And
Those hands will become a nuisance: invasive
Without you, those jokes will fall flat

And the only thing you're left begging for will be for more
than just strings keeping you far apart.

a word to the Black girls - *Yasmina Silva*

my first pick is my afro pick with a pro Black fist
for this nappy thick
and my ass thick too...

yeah, I look real cool with my natural aesthetic
but profit less than cosmetic
when the capitalists rule.

yeah, the highlight's inherent, but let's not pretend that
you like it better when
Black girls do it first...
'cause you been laughing at my skin, while filling vials with
        melanin
for how much they be selling it?
like I ain't do all the work.
i know my worth.
don't feel the verse, and throw out the words
cause this truth is hurt.
but also impossibly nuanced.

i read scripture,
paint and
t-tuh-twerk
all while teaching little Black girls
how to navigate this world
that don't seem to ever want 'em.

like how my mama teach me to be a Black woman
like how her mama learned how to become one.
powerful enough even to threaten systems and isms that need
    us broken.
we've spoken,
over and over and
over again
of the struggle we're born in
but this Black girl blues ain't stolen our joy
we've proven it
        mostly to ourselves
(and whoever else is really listening)

but we told 'em
this Black girl magic saucy, drip-dripping
and ain't that something
this existence
winning at every intersection
mother Maya said it
we rising
how many times you say Black girl in conversation?

my body language hella repetitive with it (Black girl)
poetic with it (Black girl)
step into the room and be yelling with it (Black girl)
it's lit (Black girl)
like make sure you acknowledging this Black girl
can't be getting sick of us Black girls
not when you profit from us Black girls

listen to the Black girls
we ain't voiceless just unmute us a bit
we louder than you ever would have imagined it

imagine this
gravity is like a myth to us
we elevated
our God is lifting us
pretending we not there is getting dangerous
cause we'll leave silently and take the magic with us
and then what?
                              what's a body without a spine?
what is left of you
when it was always all mine?
like,
you can scar my body fifty-four different times
displace me from mama house
and i'll still find my tribe
keep in mind a whole village took part in raising me
like
        that's my daughter too
this love story among Black women is truly the most
        beautiful
don't at me like you got a clue
of what we're surviving through
of what we have done for you
we don't forget the measures we've taken to
hold on to mama Africa's native tongue
and truth.

can't never stray too far from these roots
when teaching these fruits
how to handle these bruises
that they living through
the same lessons life taught us too
but enjoy it Black girl you're wonderful
and they won't ever be through hunting you
but your God ain't done loving you,
i'll be loving you
like how my mama keep loving me too,
keep loving me through,
so keep loving your truth.

it's a word.

Nomad - *Zeddie*

I came home to you,
With open arms' wide eyed and seeking forgiveness
I came to you,
Renewed and stronger - now I am older
I came home to you
Ready
Willing to sow seeds and produce fruit within the barren fields
I came to you with a gift
Though, 'twas unwrapped and unkept
we made the best of the situations we were in
It was a peace treaty in which you turned into a sacrifice
Now I return empty handed
With battles brewing in hot pots
Tears overflowing with desperation questions and frustration
With stained sheets and lucid dreams
Imploding in the silence
While she sleeps
There is no pause no undo
Just broken gifts
bodies bound eyes closed
Searching in the dark again
Now Things are worse than they started

ACKNOWLEDGEMENTS

Thank you, God.

Thank you to these utter gems in my life for listening, being there for the break downs, holding me up, the laughs, the honesty, for being the constants in my life:
Kasim
Sabeeka
Lexia
Carl
Tish

Thank you to Stuart and Verve Poetry Press for being patient and generous.
Thank you Amerah Saleh for being there from the beginning.
Thank you to Joelle Taylor for manoeuvring me safely through the writing process, for helping with editing, for making me feel less alone.
Thank you to Sabrina Mahfouz for always giving me time.
Thank you to my family, especially my cousins, for ongoing support.
Thank you to all the inspiring and resilient women in my life, some who have inspired certain poems.
Thank you to my Twisted Tongues team and family – Dan, Ben, Robbie, Tom
Thank you to all my Mouthy Poets family, this book began as ideas at Nottingham Playhouse during our Friday sessions. Big up Anne Holloway, Debris Stevenson, Nikki Disney and Charlotte Hodkinson.
Thank you to Sammy Joe for the courage, rest softly.

Thank you to Shaw Hill and Park View Schools for helping mould my creativity.

Thank you to all my lecturers at University of Derby.

Thank you to Adam Bushell-Jones for the cover design.

Thank you to everyone at DBT with Forward Thinking B'ham for helping to keep me well.

Thank you to Carys Hannah for being a top bab and a top friend.

Thank you to Harvi Kang for being near enough a sister.

Thank you to Yasmina Silva, Mina Mekic and Zeddie for your words.

Thank you to Derby Theatre, MAC Birmingham, and Birmingham Rep for the growth.

Thank you to Nigel.

Thank you to Alisha.

Thank you to Martin, for always challenging me, for the learning. For staying up past midnight listening to my new poems and offering up advice from a non-poet's perspective.

Thank you Ntozake Shange, for where it all began: For Colored Girls who have Considered Suicide/ When The Rainbow is Enuf (1975)

Thank you, the reader, for buying this book, for holding me, for giving me space, for the listening and understanding.

Thank you to Derby, Nottingham and Bristol for letting me escape.

Thank you to Birmingham for always welcoming me home. You will always be home.

England/ Pakistan.

...

Mud Press (mudpress.co.uk): Woman

Saqi Books: The Things I would Tell You, British Muslim Women Write

ABOUT VERVE POETRY PRESS

Verve Poetry Press is a new press focussing initially on meeting a local need in Birmingham - a need for the vibrant poetry scene here in Brum to find a way to present itself to the poetry world via publication. Co-founded by Stuart Bartholomew and Amerah Saleh, it will be publishing poets this year from all corners of the city - poets that represent the city's varied and energetic qualities and will communicate its many poetic stories.

As well as this wonderful collection from Nafeesa - look out in 2018 for stunning first collections from Amerah, Casey Bailey Leon Priestnall, Rupinder Kaur, Kamil Mahmood and Hannah Swings, to name but a few. And watch this new press bring the colour and attitude of Verve Poetry Festival, our sister in Birmingham based poetry activity, to all its publishing and event-making.

Like the festival, we will strive to think about poetry in inclusive ways and embrace the multiplicity of approaches towards this glorious art.

So watch this space. Verve Poetry Press has arrived!

www.vervepoetrypress.com
@VervePoetryPres
mail@vervepoetrypress.com